What Is the Story of Transformers?

by Brandon T. Snider

illustrated by Ted Hammond

Penguin Workshop

For Terry and Jean—BTS

To my kids, Stephanie and Jason—TH

PENGUIN WORKSHOP
An imprint of Penguin Random House LLC, New York

First published in the United States of America by Penguin Workshop,
an imprint of Penguin Random House LLC, New York, 2022

Visit us online at penguinrandomhouse.com.

Library of Congress Cataloging-in-Publication Data is available.

Printed in the United States of America

ISBN 9780593384923 (paperback)   10 9 8 7 6 5 4 3 2 1 WOR
ISBN 9780593384930 (library binding)   10 9 8 7 6 5 4 3 2 1 WOR

Contents

What Is the Story of Transformers?

In 1983, executives from the Hasbro toy company traveled to Japan on a mission to find the next great toy. They wanted something that sparked the imagination and had the potential to become a big success in the United States and around the world. What they found at the Tokyo Toy Show were two distinct kinds of toys made by a company named Takara. The first was Diaclone, a series of human-operated vehicles that converted into robots. The second was Microman, a series of real-world objects that changed into small robots. By simply shifting their moving parts, the Diaclone and Microman robots became two toys in one! The robots had curious names, like Battle Convoy and Cassette Machine Battlebike. They were impressive, with a sleek design that kids were sure to fall in love with.

These robots were so new and different that Hasbro couldn't help but think of all the exciting possibilities they could create around them. But something seemed to be missing. Who were these dynamic, changeable robots? Did they come from outer space or were they created by human beings? What was their mission? And, most importantly: Did they have a story to tell?

Diaclone robots

The Hasbro company had a lot of work to do if they wanted to turn their new discovery into a success. Little did anyone know that one day in the near future, these changing robots would take the world by storm through toys, animation, comic books, and movies. But first they needed the right story.

CHAPTER 1
Robots in Disguise

Hasbro had found what they were looking for and couldn't wait to bring their discovery back to the United States. Takara-Tomy's changing robots were perfect for the American toy market. Each robot had been expertly crafted by a passionate team of designers overseen by a man named Hideaki Yoke. The Takara-Tomy team was thrilled to have their work appreciated by such a well-respected company and looked forward to seeing what Hasbro would do with their creations. It was time to get to work.

Everyone at Hasbro knew that without an

Hideaki Yoke

exciting story for the changing robots, their new discovery might never become the hit they hoped it would be. Executives turned to Marvel Comics and together worked hard to envision a sensational origin story that would draw kids into the world of what were now called Transformers robots. Marvel Comics editor in chief Jim Shooter had a big job ahead of him and, knowing he couldn't do it alone, hired creators Denny O'Neil and Bob Budiansky to help develop this brand-new universe of characters. What they came up with was a legend of epic proportions!

Jim Shooter with Denny O'Neil and Bob Budiansky

Hideaki Yoke

Hideaki Yoke joined Takara-Tomy in 1977 and helped create Diaclone and Microman toys. He designed Diaclone's Battle Convoy, the basis for what would become Optimus Prime, and worked with Hasbro to bring the Transformers robots to the United States. Yoke had a keen eye for how the toys changed from robot to vehicle. Each one was like a puzzle that needed solving. One of his favorite characters was the Autobot scientist called Perceptor, who changed into a microscope.

In 2009, animators created a wise old Autobot named Yoketron as a way to honor Yoke's work. In 2010, Yoke was inducted into the Transformers Hall of Fame along with another toy designer, named Kohjin Ohno. He retired in 2017.

It all began with two warring groups of robots, the heroic Autobots and the evil Decepticons, who were locked in battle on the faraway world of Cybertron. With the planet's resources drained, their fuel—glowing cubes known as Energon— was in very short supply. The Cybertronians needed to find new sources of Energon in order to survive.

Cybertron

Ark spaceship

The Autobots boarded their Ark spaceship and launched into the cosmos looking for help. Tragically, they never found it. They crash-landed on Earth over four million years ago. With their systems off-line and their ship stuck at the bottom of a volcano, this seemed like the end of the Autobots and Decepticons. But their story was far from over. The Cybertronians woke from their long sleep in the present and found themselves on a strange new world. With no way home, the Autobots formed an alliance with the humans, gathered Energon, and prepared to return to Cybertron, all while fighting off Decepticon attacks.

With the basic story complete, Bob Budiansky was given a very important mission. He and the team at Marvel had to create names and personality profiles for each of the twenty-six Cybertronians—and fast! Hasbro wanted to launch Transformers as soon as possible. Budiansky got to work, and the characters soon took shape in his imagination.

The Autobots would be led by a dutiful soldier named Optimus Prime, who changed into a semitruck. Optimus Prime was a courageous hero who surrounded himself with trusted friends like special operations expert Jazz, who changed into a race car, and a young scout named Bumblebee, who changed into a Volkswagen Beetle.

Optimus Prime

Jazz and Bumblebee

The Decepticons would bow before a fearsome warrior named Megatron, who changed into a laser blaster. Megatron brought terror to all those who opposed him and often relied on his

communications expert, Soundwave, to advise
him of secret Autobot plans. Soundwave changed
into a boom box that played cassette tapes. Other
Decepticons schemed to challenge Megatron's
power, like his power-hungry second-in-command,
Starscream, who changed into a fighter jet.

Megatron and Starscream

In a matter of days, Budiansky and his team of creators had given the Autobots and Decepticons individual personalities.

Now that the Transformers' characters were fully developed, an animated commercial was made by a company called Griffin-Bacal.

This action-packed advertisement sparked people's interest. It even had a unique jingle that let people know these were no ordinary vehicles; they were something much more mysterious: "Transformers: More Than Meets the Eye! Robots in Disguise!" The catchy tagline awakened kids' curiosity and, when Transformers toys finally arrived in stores across North America in the spring of 1984, they were an instant success.

Each robot came with a unique biography— their individual life story—that was printed on its packaging. All the elements had come together and the story of the Cybertronians, one of survival, determination, and partnership, had just begun to unfold.

CHAPTER 2
More Than Meets the Eye

On May 8, 1984, Marvel Comics launched *The Transformers*, a comic book that told the story

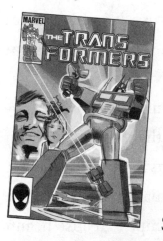

of war between Autobots and Decepticons both on Earth and on their home planet of Cybertron. It was written by Bill Mantlo, Ralph Macchio, and Jim Salicrup, with art by Frank Springer.

The Transformers comic built upon the Cybertronians' world by developing the characters and their relationships with one another. Leader Optimus Prime is a respected figure who makes tough decisions in the face of danger. He is a courageous robot who inspires his fellow Autobots to greatness. Megatron, on the other hand, is a fearsome commander who divides the Decepticons in his quest for ultimate power. He's also insecure. With treacherous deputies like Starscream and Soundwave, who can blame him? Megatron's prideful ways always put him in danger of being overthrown.

The Transformers often told stories that showed the reader what it was really like to live in a world filled with gigantic robots fighting for survival. The series also introduced the Creation Matrix, a clever means by which Autobots and Decepticons reproduced. Housed within the heart of the Autobot leader, this device contains the power to bring new Cybertronians to life. It's a mysterious and unexplained force that evolved over time. Renamed as the Matrix of Leadership, it became a glowing crystal orb encased in a metal shell with handles on either side. The Matrix grew to become a very important part of Cybertronian history.

The Matrix of Leadership

The Transformers comic book was notable for one of its special guest stars: Marvel Comics' very own Spider-Man. It wouldn't be the last crossover for the heroes of Cybertron. Later, Marvel published *G.I. Joe and the Transformers*, a story in which the Autobots teamed up with G.I. Joe, another popular Hasbro toy.

Together, they stopped the evil alliance of Cobra and the Decepticons from destroying the world with an energy drill.

On September 17, 1984, four months after their comic book debut, *The Transformers* animated series began airing on TV screens across the United States. The voice cast included Peter Cullen as Optimus Prime, Frank Welker as Megatron, and musician Scatman Crothers as Jazz, among others.

Peter Cullen

The three-part episode "More Than Meets the Eye" introduces the Autobots and Decepticons as they wake up after crash-landing on Earth millions of years ago. Adapting to their new surroundings, the Cybertronians take the form of familiar Earth vehicles, such as trucks, cars, and fighter jets. While the Autobots devote themselves to protecting humanity, the Decepticons want to drain the planet of its energy and resources. The two groups are locked in conflict, with the fate of the world hanging in the balance!

Determined to get home to Cybertron, the Autobots realize they need a helping hand if they want to achieve their goal. So they befriend a human mechanic named Sparkplug Witwicky, who helps them on missions. Sparkplug's son, a teenager named Spike, becomes best pals with Bumblebee. Building a partnership with humans is difficult for the Autobots at times, especially with the Decepticons looming around every corner.

Sparkplug and Spike Witwicky

The cast of characters grew bigger as new toys were introduced. Eye-catching robot species such as the Dinobots, Insecticons, and Constructicons became regular cast members. And on September 23, 1985, a second season of *The Transformers* began airing every weekday afternoon. Kids raced home to catch new episodes after school. They couldn't get enough of Soundwave's unique voice or the famous converting sound effect.

The Transformers animated series was a success! But one of the Cybertronians' most famous onscreen moments was still to come.

Dinobots

Frank Welker (1946–)

Frank Welker was born in Denver, Colorado, and attended Santa Monica College in California, where he studied theater arts. An American voice-over artist with over 860 film, TV, and video game credits to his name, Welker first became famous in 1969 for voicing Fred Jones on *Scooby-Doo, Where Are You!* His other notable credits include *Super Friends*, *The Smurfs*, *The Garfield Show*, and *The Simpsons*. Welker voiced many characters on *The Transformers* over the years, including Megatron, Soundwave, Skywarp, Mirage, and Trailbreaker. For his legendary voice work, Welker was inducted into the Transformers Hall of Fame in 2015.

CHAPTER 3
The Transformers: The Movie

The Hasbro company took the Cybertronians to the next level in 1986 with the big-budget animated feature film *The Transformers: The Movie.* It was directed by Nelson Shin and featured popular actors like Leonard Nimoy, Eric Idle, and Orson Welles. But this was no ordinary kids' cartoon. The movie poster read: "Beyond good. Beyond evil. Beyond your wildest imagination."

The story begins in the year 2005.

After years of war, the villainous Decepticons have conquered Cybertron and are preparing a final push to vanquish the Autobots once and for all. But the noble Autobots are ready to strike! From their hideout on Cybertron's moon, they secretly plan a counterattack to take back their home planet.

Cybertron's moon

Things change when Megatron and his minions hijack an Autobot supply ship and assault Autobot City on Earth. A fierce fight follows.

Optimus Prime goes toe-to-toe with Megatron in battle. Despite getting knocked down over and over again, Optimus Prime keeps getting back up. His fearless fighting spirit won't quit!

Sadly, when the dust settles, Optimus Prime is beyond repair. Struggling to function, he gives the Matrix of Leadership to his chief lieutenant, Ultra Magnus, and presses his fellow Autobots to keep fighting "till all are one." In an instant, the spark of life inside Optimus Prime disappears, and his body turns gray. The leader of the Autobots was gone. It was a defining moment in the history of the Transformers. Such an unexpected death left fans heartbroken and in shock.

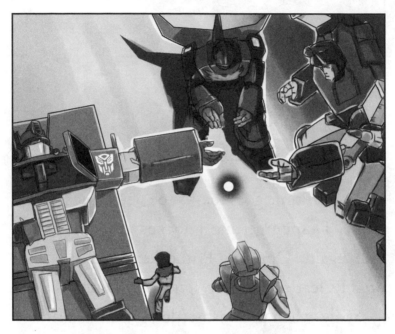

Megatron also dies in *The Transformers: The Movie* but is swiftly reborn. An enormous planet-size robot called Unicron reconstructs Megatron's lifeless body, turning him into a dangerous new Decepticon leader named Galvatron, who destroys Starscream and sets out to steal the

Matrix so he can use its power for himself. A new group of Autobots, like Springer, Arcee, and Kup stands against him, but when the Autobots stare down their darkest hour, all hope resides in an inexperienced and overconfident robot named Hot Rod. He unlocks the power of the Matrix of Leadership and uses it to destroy Unicron before the world-eating menace consumes Cybertron.

Unicron

In doing so, Hot Rod powers up to become the new commander of the Autobots, Rodimus Prime. A new day dawns, and a new chapter begins for the citizens of Cybertron.

The third season of *The Transformers* animated

series picks up where the movie left off as the Autobots work to restore Cybertron as a symbol of hope in the galaxy. It is a very difficult job. Not only has Galvatron become unstable in his quest for power, but an ancient race of evil aliens called the Quintessons rise to challenge the Autobots' efforts.

A Quintesson

Rodimus Prime tries his best to be the leader the Autobots need but sometimes the burden of leadership is too much for him to bear.

New Class

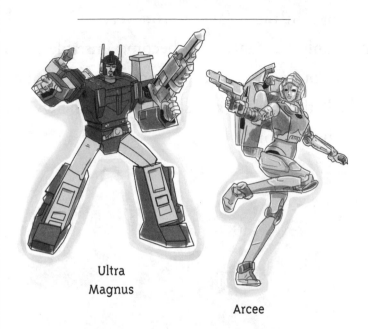

Ultra
Magnus

Arcee

Ultra Magnus is a dependable Autobot soldier who follows orders and supports his teammates. No matter the risk, you can always count on Ultra Magnus to get the job done. Arcee is the first featured female Autobot to be included in *The Transformers* cast. She's an expert fighter and a skilled sharpshooter who uses her wits to get out of dangerous situations. Springer is a triple changer, which means he can become a robot, a land vehicle, and a helicopter. He's also a brave warrior with a sense of humor, which keeps things light when darkness creeps in. Kup is the tough veteran of the bunch. He's seen a lot of combat over his many years. The other Autobots jokingly say that Kup is as old as rust.

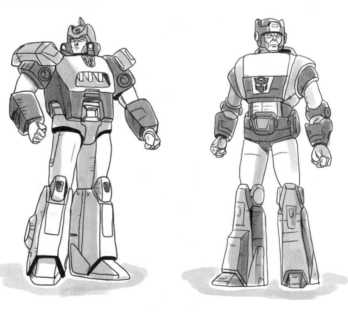

Springer   Kup

Help soon arrives in the form of an old friend. Fans missed Optimus Prime so much that they organized a letter-writing campaign hoping to bring him back. Hasbro heard them loud and clear. In a special two-part episode, "The Return of Optimus Prime," the greatest leader of the Autobots is brought back to life to stop a plague of hate from destroying the universe. With Optimus Prime's return, the Autobots are reenergized and ready to expand their ranks.

CHAPTER 4
Generation 2

Following their film appearance, the Transformers bots continued to change both on toy shelves and on television. As one of the top toy companies in the world, Hasbro knew that innovation was the key to keeping the brand creative and fresh. From 1987 to 1990, each new set of Transformers bots had a unique feature unlike any that had come before.

Targetmasters were regular-size Transformers bots who partnered with a small companion robot that converted into a weapon. Headmasters partnered with a companion robot that transformed into the head of the larger robot. Powermasters were bonded to a power supply while Micromasters were human-size robots.

Actionmasters were Transformers bots who'd
lost their ability to transform and relied on
converting vehicles in battle. Pretenders hid their
robot bodies inside a humanoid or animal-like
shell.

Even with so many impressive additions to the Transformers universe over the years, the original lineup of Autobots and Decepticons remained wildly popular. Hasbro took note and in 1993, they made a big comeback as the new and improved Transformers: Generation 2. This time around, classic Transformers bots had updated designs and brand-new logos. Some characters looked the same but with bright new paint jobs. Others, like Megatron, were reborn in completely new forms.

Megatron from Generation 2

Since attitudes had changed toward selling lifelike guns as toys, Megatron was now a camouflage tank. Cool action-oriented features were added to each toy, such as launching weapons, sound chips, and water-shooting cannons. The Autobot and Decepticon symbols were also given a sleek new redesign as part of the brand makeover. Transformers fans were so excited to see their favorite characters back, they started their own convention, called BotCon.

BotCon

The first BotCon was held in Fort Wayne, Indiana, in 1994. This convention, organized by the Official Transformers Collectors' Club, featured booths where fans could buy toys, comics, and film memorabilia.

BotCon hosted voice actors from the animated series who talked about their work. It was also the place to find unofficial and exclusive Transformers toys and comic books made especially for the event. To honor the many creators, artists, and other individuals who have made an impact on the world of Transformers, BotCon started the Transformers Hall of Fame in 2012.

Joining this new line of toys was a twelve-issue *Transformers: Generation 2* comic book series, written by Simon Furman with art by Derek Yaniger, published by Marvel Comics. The stories were more adventurous than what was seen in the *Transformers* comic books that came before. The series begins with Optimus Prime haunted by a grim vision he receives from the Matrix. With the Autobots exhausted by endless war with the Decepticons, there would be no time for rest. New threats arise in the form of an old Cybertronian named Jhiaxus and a mass of black energy known as the Swarm. Only by forming an alliance are the Autobots and Decepticons able to reach an uneasy peace.

After *Transformers: Generation 2* ended in 1995, it was time for something new and unexpected. And Hasbro had the perfect plan. On the horizon was a bold, eye-catching metamorphosis—a new type of transformation—that would change the brand forever.

CHAPTER 5
Beast Wars: Transformers

In 1996, Transformers underwent one of their most daring changes to date. Together with Takara, Hasbro designed a brand-new line of robot toys. The vehicular designs of the past were gone! Now the Cybertronians changed into beastly animal forms. With an original animated series set on a strange new world, this was the era known as *Beast Wars: Transformers*.

The story begins three hundred years in the future, where the heroic Maximals are in pursuit of the villainous Predacons. Both warring clans crash-land on a faraway planet where the Energon is poisonous. To protect themselves from dangerous radiation, the Predacons and the Maximals adopt techno-organic outer shells

Predacons and Maximals crash-landing

that cover their Cybertronian forms. On the outside, they may have animal-like fur, feathers, or reptilian skin but on the inside, they are all robots. Their disguises help them blend into their new surroundings.

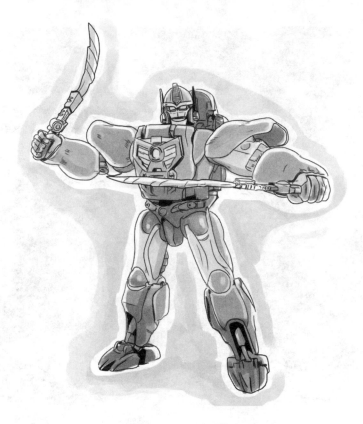

Optimus Primal

Leading the Maximals is Optimus Primal, who changes into a mighty gorilla. It is difficult for him to juggle his animal temper with the demands of leadership, and he often struggles with his role as commander. Other Maximals include Cheetor, an energetic young robot who is fast on his feet, and Rattrap, a sarcastic jokester with a knack for surveillance.

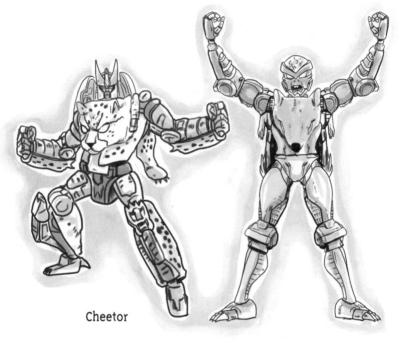

Cheetor

Rattrap

Leading the Predacons is a criminal called Megatron, who stole his name from the "great destroyer" mentioned in an old Cybertronian text. Megatron is a devious boss who changes into a menacing *Tyrannosaurus rex*. He is joined by Predacons such as the spiderlike double agent, Blackarachnia, and the fiercely loyal Scorponok.

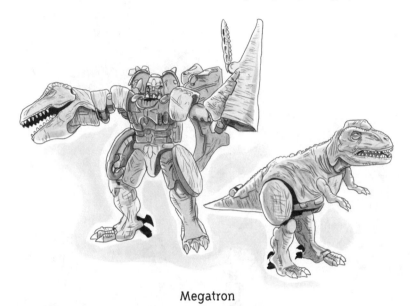

Megatron

With a style unlike any previous *Transformers* series, *Beast Wars: Transformers* featured cutting-edge CGI animation. The series was notable for showing that each Cybertronian had a unique personality and perspective. Stories had humor and heart, but they could also be serious.

Scorponok

Blackarachnia

In one memorable episode called "Code of Hero," a robot named Dinobot is forced to make a difficult choice. At first, Dinobot joins the Predacons thinking they can bring him power and glory, but when he challenges Megatron's leadership, things don't go exactly as planned.

Dinobot

The Predacon leader laughs in his face. This makes Dinobot so angry he switches sides, sharing insider knowledge of the Predacons' evil plans with the Maximals. Though Optimus Primal is suspicious at times, he welcomes Dinobot's help with open arms.

But their alliance is short-lived. Dinobot switches sides whenever the moment suits him. Over time, his shifty behavior leaves him feeling conflicted about himself. Is he good or bad? Is he honorable or crooked at heart? When Megatron threatens to change history with a powerful Cybertronian artifact called the Golden Disk, Dinobot sacrifices himself to stop him.

Dinobot destroys the Golden Disk

It is an act of bravery that earns him a special place in Cybertronian history. Before he dies, Dinobot makes peace with his troubled past and asks the Maximals to tell his story truthfully—the good and the bad. In the end, his actions are those of an honorable warrior.

In *Beast Machines: Transformers*, the 1999 sequel series, the Maximals are back on war-torn Cybertron and stuck in their animal forms with no memory of their past. What could be worse? How about Megatron using his legion of mindless Vehicon drones to hunt the Maximals down and capture them? Optimus Primal and his team have to adapt in order to avoid being caught. So with the help of a powerful supercomputer called Oracle, the Maximals level up into newer beastly forms. Together, they defeat Megatron, free the people of Cybertron, and bring life to the planet once again.

The Oracle

This series, which ended in 2000, had a much gloomier tone than *Beast Wars: Transformers* as the Transformers bots discovered the truth behind the history of Cybertron. While *Beast Wars: Transformers* introduced the concept of the Spark, an energy source that represents the soul of a Cybertronian, *Beast Machines: Transformers* introduced the AllSpark, the source of all robotic life. The AllSpark grew to become very important to the Transformers universe in years to come.

Pure Power

The AllSpark is a silver metallic cube covered in ancient symbols called cyberglyphs that can bring new Transformers bots to life. Its energy is believed to be responsible for creating the planet Cybertron.

Though its exact history is unknown, the AllSpark is an object of incredible power that has been around for centuries. It's so powerful that even if its outer shell is destroyed, pieces of the AllSpark energy would remain. The Autobots have fought valiantly over the years to keep the Decepticons from possessing the AllSpark, even launching it into space to protect it from harm.

CHAPTER 6
The Unicron Trilogy

The Transformers bots returned to television in 2002 sporting fresh looks in a brand-new animated series called *Transformers: Armada*. It was produced by both Hasbro and Takara and had a dynamic animation style. The style, known as anime, was very popular in Japan, but this was the first time American audiences had seen the Transformers bots in such a way. Fans found the series original and exciting. In Japan, the show was known as *Super Robot Life-Form Transformers: Legends of the Microns*.

The story of *Transformers: Armada* finds the Autobots and Decepticons locked in battle over a race of smaller, power-enhancing robots called

Mini-Cons. The Mini-Cons are human-size bots that bond to larger Cybertronian bots. This gives them both a big boost of energy called a Power Link.

Characters from *Super Robot Life-Form Transformers: Legends of the Microns*

Mini-Cons Grindor, High Wire, and Sureshock

In the distant past, during Cybertron's Great War, the Mini-Cons built a spaceship and rocketed away to safety with the help of the Autobots. But the Decepticons weren't far behind. They followed the Mini-Cons and destroyed their ship, causing it to crash-land on Earth. Millions of years later, humans discover the wreckage of the

Mini-Cons' ship, and in doing so, accidentally send a signal into space summoning the other Cybertronians to their location.

Mini-Cons' ship flying in Earth's atmosphere

Optimus Prime and Megatron soon arrive on Earth alongside their teammates and the search for the Mini-Cons begins. It is later revealed that the villainous Unicron created the Mini-Cons as a way to cause conflict between the Autobots and

Decepticons. The more they fight, the stronger Unicron becomes! Only by joining together are the Cybertronians able to defeat Unicron. *Transformers: Armada* was the first of three animated series that would come to be called *The Unicron Trilogy*.

Unicron

The 2004 series *Transformers: Energon* picks up the story ten years later. Things are peaceful on Cybertron and on Earth. But it doesn't last long.

Alpha Quintesson

A mysterious alien called the Alpha Quintesson comes up with an evil plan to bring Unicron back to life. Using Unicron's robotic remains, the Alpha Quintesson builds an army of mindless, Energon-eating robots called Terrorcons. These beastly drones cause terror and destruction wherever they go, attacking Autobot cities across the galaxy.

The Autobots are quite busy after Megatron returns and takes over the body of Omega Supreme, one of the Guardians of Cybertron. Optimus Prime combines his power with that of Omega Supreme, one of the Guardians of Cybertron, and together they become a giant robot warrior called Optimus Supreme. With the help of his Autobot comrades, Optimus Supreme is able to turn the tide of battle and win the day.

Optimus Supreme

In the final part of the trilogy, 2005's *Transformers: Cybertron*, a giant black hole threatens to swallow Cybertron. Only a device called the Omega Lock can save the planet. But without the Cyber Planet Keys to open it, the Omega Lock is not useful. So the Autobots jump into action to secure the keys. As always, the Decepticons are right behind them.

Returning to Cybertron with the keys in hand, the Autobots open the Omega Lock and awaken the sleeping Primus, god of all Cybertronians. body is made from Cybertron itself! But Megatr also gets his hands on one of the keys and uses its power to transform himself into Galvatron. After Primus uses the keys to seal the black hole, Optimus Prime defeats Galvatron and watches his enemy dissolve into space dust. Finally at peace, the Autobots build a space bridge and venture out into the universe where new adventures await.

Primus

CHAPTER 7
Return to Greatness

By 2006, it had been many years since the original Transformers robots had been seen. Nostalgia is the warm feeling you get from a past memory, and fans felt very nostalgic for Optimus Prime, Megatron, and the cast of characters they grew up with. IDW Publishing jumped at the chance to bring back everyone's favorite robots  from Generation 1, and they soon began publishing a new comic book series that officially started the Hasbro Comic Book Universe.

Transformers: Infiltration, written by Simon Furman with art by E. J. Su, not only brought back the original Autobots and Decepticons but it gave them a brand-new origin as well. Instead of crash-landing on Earth, the Cybertronians arrive as undercover agents, living among humans in secret as "robots in disguise." But when a secret government agency called the Machination forces the Autobots and Decepticons out of hiding, the robots form an alliance with humanity in order to survive.

After *Transformers: Infiltration*, IDW published a variety of *Transformers* comic books that continued

The Machination

the Cybertronians' adventures in space and on Earth. *Transformers: Spotlight* told individual stories about Cybertronians who hadn't been

given a chance to shine before, like Shockwave, Blaster, Metroplex, and Cyclonus, and *Transformers: Megatron Origin* told the secret history of one of the most infamous robots on Cybertron as he went from humble Energon miner to fearsome leader of the Decepticons. Some stories were big action-packed adventures, while others were quiet character-driven tales.

In the story *Transformers: Chaos Theory*, Optimus Prime and Megatron are forced to confront their past when it's revealed that before they were bitter enemies, they had been friends!

In their younger days, when Optimus r
was a police captain, he and Megatron foug
Cybertron's crooked leaders together. But their
relationship changed over millions of years and,
eventually, they became rivals.

Tensions erupted during the Great War when
Optimus Prime and Megatron were forced to
make difficult choices they thought were right.
Some of those choices end up costing the Autobots
and Decepticons dearly. By the end of the story,
Optimus Prime and Megatron understand each
other in a new way, though neither apologizes

neir past choices. Years of conflict have made
.em stubborn. After their conversation, Optimus
Prime decides it's time to step back from his role
as Autobot commander to do some soul-searching
and leave Cybertron. This sets the stage for the
next wave of stories to come.

In *Transformers: More Than Meets the Eye*,
written by James Roberts with art by Alex
Milne and others, Cybertron is at peace. But a
young thrill-seeking Autobot named Rodimus
Prime has his eye on exploring the cosmos. So
he assembles a crew and blasts off into space in
search of a group of peace-loving Cybertronians
called the Knights of Cybertron. Aboard his ship,
the *Lost Light*, Rodimus Prime and his comrades
encounter all kinds of trouble along the way.
Their adventures continue in *Transformers: Lost
Light*, written by James Roberts with art by Jack
Lawrence and others. In this story, team Rodimus
Prime ends up stranded on a dark cemetery

planet called Necroworld. The only hope
have of returning home is a group of time
traveling Cybertronians called the Disappeared.
An explosion sends Rodimus Prime and his crew
to an entirely different universe!

Rodimus Prime

On this new twisted world, Megatron had never been born and Cybertronian history was completely different. But team Rodimus Prime rises to the occasion, using their wits, wisdom, and fighting skills to save the day and return to Cybertron safely.

IDW's new *Transformers* comic books were a hit with fans, and the *Transformers* animated TV series was as popular as ever. But the success the brand soon found on movie screens would propel them to new heights of popularity around the world.

Allies Reunited

Written by John Barber with art by Tom Scioli, the *Transformers vs. G.I. Joe* comic book series reunited the two popular Hasbro brands but with a clever twist. In this new universe, the Autobots and G.I. Joe meet for the very  first time! When Cybertron enters Earth's solar system, the Decepticons demand that humans surrender to them or else. G.I. Joe teams up with the Autobots to stop the invasion but uncover a secret in the process: Earth and Cybertron had been connected for a very long time. Optimus Prime and Megatron face off as G.I. Joe defeats the forces of Cobra.

CHAPTER 8
Transformers Reborn

In 2007, executive producer Steven Spielberg and director Michael Bay teamed up to bring the Autobots and Decepticons to the big screen in a new live-action *Transformers* movie. Animators used state-of-the-art CGI to craft brand-new looks for Optimus Prime, Megatron, Bumblebee, and others. Instead of their classic robot forms,

Steven Spielberg

Michael Bay

the Autobots and Decepticons were now mac
sleek, organic-looking steel. They had express
mouths and faces that made them look like
humans instead of robots. Fans couldn't believe
their eyes! Their favorite characters looked like
nothing they'd seen before.

The *Transformers* movie features a story well
known to fans. On Cybertron, the Autobots and
Decepticons are at war over the AllSpark. To
keep it safe, Optimus Prime launches it into
space, away from the Decepticons. But Megatron
doesn't give up so easily. He chases the AllSpark
through the cosmos, crash-landing on Earth
alongside it.

Thousands of years later, in the present day, Decepticons come to Earth looking for their long-lost leader.

Sam Witwicky

Instead, they find a young man named Sam Witwicky, who unknowingly holds the key to finding the AllSpark. As the Decepticons attack Sam, his new car changes into a giant robot named Bumblebee. A Cybertronian in disguise, Bumblebee rescues Sam and introduces him to

Optimus Prime and the Autobots. Together,
stop Megatron from using the AllSpark to cont
the planet's machinery and destroy the human
race.

Sam meets the Autobots

Having saved the planet, Optimus Prime and the Autobots make Earth their new home, vowing to protect humans from future harm. Audiences loved the movie's action-packed car chases, explosions, and special effects. *Transformers* earned over $700 million worldwide, and the Cybertronians' film adventures were just getting started.

In the second *Transformers* movie, 2c

Transformers: Revenge of the Fallen, a dark sec.

from the past comes to light. The first Decepticon,

now known as the Fallen, returns with a vengeance.

The Fallen

His mission is to locate a powerful device called

a Star Harvester and use it to destroy Earth. The

Autobots aren't about to let that happen. They

fight the Fallen and his Decepticon allies in a

ggle that spans the entire globe. In the end, Optimus Prime destroys the Fallen and saves the world once more.

But peace didn't last very long. In 2011's *Transformers: Dark of the Moon* movie, the Autobots discover the body of their previous

leader, Sentinel Prime, on the moon. He

crashed there years ago after being chased by t

Decepticons. Optimus Prime revives him using

the Matrix of Leadership, but it's all a Decepticon

trap. The Autobots were set up! Sentinel Prime

switched sides and is now working with Megatron.

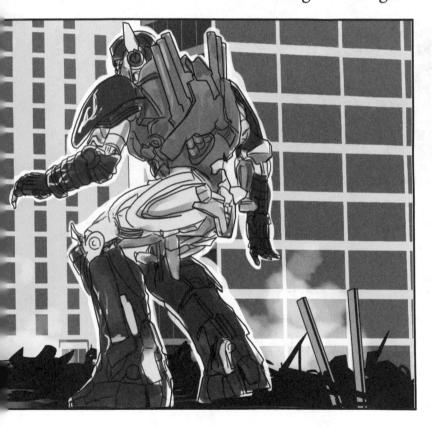

Sentinel Prime and Optimus Prime fight

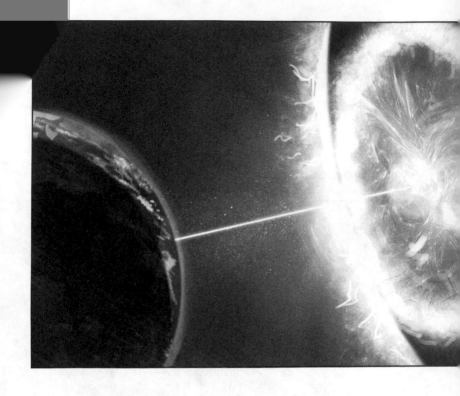

After exiling the Autobots from Earth, the Decepticons begin their takeover of the planet. Their master plan is to enslave humanity by transporting Cybertron into Earth's solar system using a space bridge. Little do they know that the Autobots set a trap of their own. They hadn't left Earth at all! They simply went into hiding.

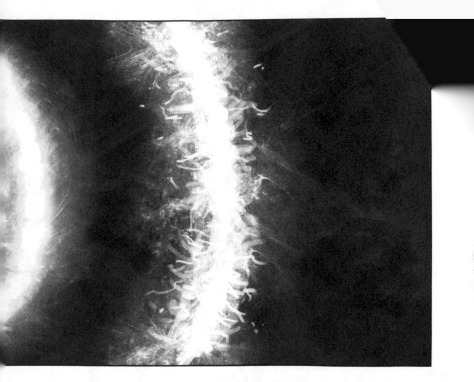

The space bridge

The Autobots and the Decepticons clash in a giant battle royale that ends with Optimus Prime destroying Megatron and Sentinel Prime along with the space bridge. Sadly, Cybertron is lost as well. With Earth saved and nowhere else to go, the Autobots disappear.

Darkness Falls

The Seven Primes were the first robots created by the AllSpark. They became the leaders of Cybertron and worked together to find worlds where they could build Solar Harvesters. These devices used the sun's energy to create Energon cubes. The Primes used Energon cubes as food and medicine. Their only rule was that they couldn't build Solar Harvesters on planets where life existed. But one of the Primes, Megatronus, broke this rule by building a Solar Harvester on Earth. Because of his great betrayal, the other Primes cast him out. He became known as the Fallen.

CHAPTER 9
The Saga Continues

The *Transformers* film series continued with 2014's *Transformers: Age of Extinction*, which introduced a new story with an all-new cast of human characters. Five years after the Cybertronians' war rocked the planet, the Autobots and Decepticons are seen as a dangerous threat to humanity. A shadowy government agency pursues them with help from a bounty hunter named Lockdown. He works for an alien race called the Creators, who had covered Earth with Seeds containing a shape-changing metal alloy called Transformium over sixty-five million years ago. The agency wants a Seed very badly and makes a deal with Lockdown to get one. All they have to do is hand over Optimus Prime.

The only problem is that Prime has gone missing. He and the Autobots are hiding from the humans. It looks as if all hope is lost until a Texas inventor named Cade Yeager discovers the old truck he'd bought is really Optimus Prime in disguise. Things take a turn for the worse when Megatron shows up in his powered-up Galvatron form. Optimus Prime and the Autobots come out of hiding to fight Lockdown and the Decepticons, alongside their new friends, the Dinobots, and end up saving the world once again.

Cade Yeager with Optimus Prime in disguise

The secret history of Cybertronians on Earth is uncovered in the 2017 movie *Transformers: The Last Knight*. In the distant past, a group of Transformers called the Knights of Iacon helped mankind for centuries. But their existence was hidden by a secret society called the Order of Witwiccans.

Steelbane, one of the Knights of Iacon

In the present day, the Autobots Decepticons are being hunted down by an government organization called the Transformer Reaction Force. Optimus Prime leaves Earth to seek help on Cybertron but when he arrives, he finds the planet has been all but destroyed. On Cybertron, an evil sorceress named Quintessa brainwashes Optimus Prime into thinking he is responsible for Cybertron's destruction. Using her dark powers, Quintessa changes Optimus Prime into Nemesis Prime and tells him to return

Quintessa changes Optimus Prime

rth to find Merlin's staff, an ancient power
urce, and bring it back to her. Nemesis Prime
does as he is told. But things get worse when he
confronts Cade Yeager and the Autobots. They
have the magical talisman Nemesis Prime needs
to complete his mission.

Old friends fight like bitter enemies until
Bumblebee shakes Optimus Prime out of his
trance and returns him to his heroic former self.
The mythical sword Excalibur is awakened as
the Knights of Iacon return to help the Autobots
defeat the Decepticons.

The 2018 movie *Transformers: Bumblebee* took the Transformers films in a brand-new direction by telling a previously unknown story set twenty years before the events of the first *Transformers* film. (This kind of story

is known as a prequel.) To the delight of fans, Optimus Prime sported his classic look from the original *Transformers* animated series! And he was played by Peter Cullen, who had famously voiced the Autobot leader many times over the years.

Transformers: Bumblebee begins on Cybertron, where war had raged between the Autobots and Decepticons for a very long time. Optimus Prime gives a young scout named B-127 an important sion. He is to go to Earth to see if it is a suitable place for the Autobots to live. B-127 blasts away in an escape pod but after a terrible Decepticon attack, he crash-lands on Earth voiceless and without his memory. B-127 realizes he has to become a regular human automobile to blend in, so he adopts the form of a Volkswagen Beetle as a disguise.

On Earth, B-127 is unknowingly gifted to a teenage girl named Charlie Watson as a birthday present. She nurses the wounded bot back to health and gives him the nickname Bumblebee. Together, they build a beautiful friendship, but danger is just around the corner. A top secret government agency called Sector 7 discovers Bumblebee's whereabouts and goes after him. The Decepticons arrive on Earth and are hot on his trail as well. With Charlie's help, Bumblebee regains his memory and fights off the Decepticons. After the battle, Charlie parts ways

Charlie and Bumblebee

with Bumblebee, who joins Optimus Prime and his fellow Autobots on Earth as a new chapter begins.

Peter Cullen (1941–)

Peter Cullen was born in the city of Montreal in the Canadian province of Quebec. He was among the first graduating class of the National Theatre School of Canada in 1963 and went on to voice hundreds of characters in film and television, including Eeyore on *Winnie the Pooh* and Monterey Jack on *Chip 'n Dale: Rescue Rangers*.

Cullen has played Optimus Prime in over thirty different *Transformers* cartoons, movies, and video games. He based the Autobot leader's voice on his brother Larry, a former Marine and one of his heroes. Larry told Peter that real heroes don't lose their temper. They listen to people around them and are tough enough to be gentle, just like Optimus Prime. Cullen was inducted into the Transformers Hall of Fame in 2010.

CHAPTER 10
A Different World

The Transformers legend is a story about survival. No matter what hardships the Autobots and Decepticons face, they always forge ahead. Sometimes that leads them to make some very difficult and surprising choices. The 2016 animated series *Transformers: Combiner Wars* follows an alternate Transformers history that begins forty years after the Great War. After many years on Earth, the Autobots and Decepticons return to Cybertron, where Optimus Prime defeats Megatron and ends their conflict permanently.

From the ashes of their old rivalry, a new partnership rises. A Council of Worlds is created, made up of both Autobots and Decepticons, that includes Rodimus Prime and Starscream.

Together, the former enemies rule Cybertro.
best they can. But trouble bubbles up with t.
rise of the Combiners, a group of Transformers
who cause death and destruction wherever they
go. A valiant Autobot named Windblade refuses
to watch her planet get torn to shreds, so she takes
matters into her own hands and heroically puts
an end to the Combiner Wars. But the danger is
far from over.

In 2017's TV series *Transformers: Titans Return*, a threat from Cybertron's distant past has resurfaced. The Titans are gigantic city-size robots that contain enormous amounts of power. After the Combiner Wars, Cybertron rebuilt itself, but peace doesn't last long. A Titan called Trypticon has returned, possessed by the ghost of Starscream.

To combat this menace, Windblade, Optimus Prime, and a few other Autobots bring an old ally back to life, a Titan called Fortress Maximus.

Honor and Duty

In 2013, Hasbro asked fans to build a brand-new character by choosing different modes, weapons, and color schemes. The end result was Windblade, the first female lead in Transformers history. Her design was revealed at San Diego Comic-Con before she starred in her own IDW comic book miniseries called *The Transformers: Windblade*. As an Autobot, Windblade takes her duty very seriously, and as Cityspeaker she has the unique ability to communicate with Titans. Windblade sees the good in others and has compassion for those who struggle. But, if confronted with evil Decepticons who refuse to yield, her Stormfall Sword comes in quite handy.

Windblade

Trypticon

Working together, they defeat Trypticon, but a new threat is born when Megatronus "the Fallen" returns to life and kills Optimus Prime. Now the Autobots have no choice but to rely on the leadership of Megatron if they want to survive what comes next.

The Fallen plans his ultimate takeover in 2018's *Transformers: Power of the Primes* TV miniseries. First, the villain claims two powerful artifacts for himself: the Enigma of Combination and the Matrix of Leadership. With the third ract, the Requiem Blaster, the Fallen can create doomsday weapon that would wipe Cybertron and all of its citizens off the map. So the Autobots and their new leader, Megatron, go on a quest to find the Requiem Blaster first.

But their journey isn't easy. The Fallen sends his followers to attack! When Megatron finally locates the Requiem Blaster, he's shocked to find that it is guarded by an Autobot named Optimus Primal, one of many honorable Cybertronians who were responsible for making sure the device never fell into the wrong hands. After Megatron explains the danger Cybertron is up against, Optimus Primal joins the Autobots and clashes with the Fallen. The high point of the story arrives when Optimus Primal inherits the Matrix of Leadership and becomes the new leader of the Autobots: Optimal Prime! Together, he and his teammates save the day, ending what comes to be called *The Prime Wars*.

CHAPTER 11
Cybertron and Beyond

Hasbro believed the key to keeping the Transformers brand fresh was combining great stories with exciting and innovative toys. With that in mind, they set out to celebrate the thirty-fifth anniversary of the Cybertronians with bold new plans that had fans buzzing with excitement.

First up was the Transformers Collaborative, a new universe where Autobots and Decepticons team up with characters from other popular brands. Sometimes elements of these brands combine with Transformers bots, creating totally new combination-characters called mash-ups. Hasbro created these new Cybertronian toys while IDW published their adventures in comic book form.

In *Transformers/Ghostbusters: Ghosts of Cybertron*, an Autobot scientist named Ectotron detects a mysterious Cybertronian distress signal coming from Earth. Optimus Prime sends him to investigate, and when he arrives in New York City, he comes face-to-face with the world-famous Ghostbusters. To blend in, Ectotron adopts  the form of the Ghostbusters' famous car, the Ecto-1, and together, he and the Ghostbusters team up to fight a group of Decepticon ghosts.

After Marty McFly returns home from his time-traveling adventures, he realizes that a small mistake he made along the way caused big problems in the present day in *Transformers/Back to the Future*. And once the Decepticons realize that they can change history for their own evil means using Marty's time machine, things only get worse. With the help of an Autobot named Gigawatt, who changes into a DeLorean car, Marty and his mentor, Doc Brown, travel through time and stop the Decepticons before they ruin history.

Even My Little Pony got in on the mash-up action! In 2020's *Transformers/My Little Pony: Friendship in Disguise!*, Queen Chrysalis casts a spell to find other Changelings and transport them to Equestria so they can team up and conquer it together. But the spell accidentally connects with a Cybertronian space bridge that yanks the Autobots and Decepticons to Equestria instead. To stop the Changelings and the Decepticons, Optimus Prime and Twilight Sparkle form an alliance that saves Equestria from falling into darkness. Hasbro celebrated the historic meeting by creating a special My Little Pony mash-up toy that was painted just like Optimus Prime. In the 2021 sequel, *Transformers/My Little Pony:*

The Magic of Cybertron, the Decepticons use the Cybertronian space bridge to drain Equestria's magic. Twilight Sparkle and her friends travel to Cybertron to stop them but unexpectedly bring the evil King Sombra back to life. Only with the help of Optimus Prime and the Autobots are the ponies able to stop King Sombra's takeover.

Honoring the Cybertronians' long and famous history, each of the new Transformers toys has its own unique spin. Transformers: Shattered Glass imagines a world where Decepticons are heroes and Autobots are villains. Megatron is Cybertron's champion and Optimus Prime is an evil overlord with his eye on conquering Earth. And for fans who loved the classic bots, Hasbro created Transformers: Generations, an assortment of premium figures featuring characters from every era of Cybertronian history. From the original lineup of bots in Generation 1 to the wild animals of Beast Wars, there's something for everyone. Each bot in this line has an updated design, plus new weapons and features.

Then Hasbro took things to the next level with an innovative bot that was the first-ever electronic, voice-activated Optimus Prime, who punched, kicked, and changed into his semitruck mode on command. This premium figure was the perfect addition to fan collections.

In the animated world, the Cybertronians' historic journey to Earth was reimagined in 2020's *Transformers: War for Cybertron Trilogy*, a three-part series that shook up the Transformers universe. *War for Cybertron: Siege* begins after years of endless war on Cybertron. With the planet in ruins, the Autobots and Decepticons have exhausted their resources. As the planet grows weaker, Megatron hatches a daring plan to bring together all the Cybertronians under his rule. With the AllSpark, Megatron can reprogram the Autobots and turn them into Decepticons.

But first he has to find it. In a race against time, the Autobots try desperately to stop the Decepticons from claiming the AllSpark for themselves. In the end, Optimus Prime makes the toughest decision of his life. In order to save Cybertron, he tosses the AllSpark through a space bridge before leaving the planet aboard the Ark.

In *War for Cybertron: Earthrise*, Cybertron is under the control of Megatron. With Optimus Prime gone, the Decepticon leader rules over the planet with an iron fist. But a group of Autobots, led by a kindhearted warrior named Elita-1, fight to free the many Cybertronians who suffer under Megatron's command. After tracking down the location of the AllSpark, Megatron confronts Optimus Prime and battles him for control. Then, after a savage assault, the Cybertronians crash-land on prehistoric Earth, setting the stage for the Maximals and Predacons to arise in *War for Cybertron: Kingdom*.

Since their debut in 1984, the Transformers bots have sparked people's imaginations and touched their hearts. Optimus Prime wasn't just a fictional character; he was a friend and, for some, a father figure. The Autobots weren't just robots; they were shining examples of partnership and teamwork.

Transformers has been a story of heroism, survival, and rebirth told through the world of animation, film, and comic books. The Autobots and Decepticons have reinvented themselves for generations to the delight of fans young and old. Though they may have begun their life in Japan, the Transformers bots have grown to become American heroes. And with more heroism on the horizon, the best is yet to come.

World's Largest Collection

According to the Guinness World Records, AJ Ard of Eastvale, California, has the world's largest collection of Transformers memorabilia. He has

collected Transformers toys, comic books, trading cards, video games, and more. Over 3,600 items in total! AJ has even built what he calls a "Hall of Cybertron" inside his house to store it all.

His most prized possession is a rare Autobot made in Japan called Metalhawk. Ard fell in love with the *Transformers* animated series when he was a little boy growing up in Memphis, Tennessee. His favorite Transformers bot is Soundwave because he has a cool-sounding voice.

Bibliography

Cambro, Edward. "The 15 Best Transformers Stories of All Time." Screenrant, December 15, 2016. https://screenrant.com/transformers-best-stories-ever-beast-wars/.

Crucchiola, Jordan. "Here's Your Guide to the Very Complicated Mythology of the *Transformers* Universe." **Vulture**, June 23, 2017. https://www.vulture.com/2017/06/transformers-mythology-explained.html.

Delaney, Mike. "Mind-Blowing Moments in Transformers History." Fandom.com. https://www.fandom.com/articles/mind-blowing-moments-transformers-history.

Dille, Flint. **The Gamesmaster: My Life in the '80s Geek Culture Trenches with G.I. Joe, Dungeons & Dragons, and the Transformers**. Los Angeles: Rare Bird Books, 2020.

Fury, Sol. "Transformers Who's Who Hideaki Yoke & Koujin Oono on the History of Transformers." TFW2005, April 9, 2012. https://news.tfw2005.com/2012/04/09/transformers-whos-who-hideaki-yoke-koujin-oono-on-the-history-of-transformers-174774.

Hidalgo, Pablo. **Transformers Vault**. New York: Abrams, 2011.

"Largest Collection of Transformers Memorabilia." Guinness World Records. https://www.guinnessworldrecords.com/world-records/452355-largest-collection-of-transformers-memorabilia.

Sorenson, Jim. *Transformers: A Visual History*. San Francisco: VIZ Media LLC, 2019.

Stern, Tom, dir. *The Toys That Made Us*. Season 2, episode 2, "Transformers." Written by Benjamin Frost. Aired May 25, 2018, on Netflix.

Wall, Stephen. "How Much Does This Eastvale Man Love Transformers? He Counts 1,313 Ways." *Daily Bulletin*, June 6, 2017. https://www.dailybulletin.com/2017/06/06/how-much-does-this-eastvale-man-love-transformers-he-counts-1313-ways/.

Walsh, Ben. "How Robots Have Transformed History and You Had No Idea." *Independent*, June 23, 2017. https://www.independent.co.uk/arts-entertainment/films/transformers/how-robots-have-transformed-history-and-you-had-no-idea-a7797521.html.

Webb, Martin. "Toys That Transformed the World's Way of Play." *Japan Times*, March 19, 2006. https://www.japantimes.co.jp/life/2006/03/19/to-be-sorted/toys-that-transformed-the-worlds-way-of-play/.

Websites

Transformers.hasbro.com

YouTube.com/TransformersOfficial